W9-AYO-555

A Bit
Is a Bite

Written by Larry Dane Brimner
Illustrated by Erin Eitter Kono

Children's Press®
A Division of Scholastic Inc.
New York • Toronto • London • Auckland • Sydney
Mexico City • New Delhi • Hong Kong
Danbury, Connecticut

For Carson and Cassidy Brimner.
—L. D. B.

For Caitlyn Akiko.
—E. E. K.

Reading Consultant

Cecilia Minden-Cupp, PhD
Former Director of the Language and Literacy Program
Harvard Graduate School of Education
Cambridge, Massachusetts

Cover design: The Design Lab
Interior design: Herman Adler

Library of Congress Cataloging-in-Publication Data

Brimner, Larry Dane.
  A Bit is a bite / by Larry Dane Brimner; illustrated by Erin Eitter Kono.
      p. cm. — (Rookie reader: silent letters)
    ISBN-13: 978-0-531-17547-7 (lib. bdg.)   978-0-531-17780-8 (pbk.)
    ISBN-10: 0-531-17547-2 (lib. bdg.)   0-531-17780-7 (pbk.)
  1. English language—Vowels—Juvenile literature. I. Kono, Erin
Eitter. II. Title. III. Series.
  PE1157.B75 2007
  428.1'3—dc22   2006024388

CHILDREN'S PRESS, and A ROOKIE READER®, and associated logos
are trademarks and/or registered trademarks of Scholastic Library
Publishing. SCHOLASTIC and associated logos are trademarks and/or
registered trademarks of Scholastic Inc.
1 2 3 4 5 6 7 8 9 10 R 16 15 14 13 12 11 10 09 08 07

"Dad, please don't be mad!"

"I know I slid down the rail."

"The rail isn't a slide."

"I guess I ate more than a bit of cake."

"A bit is a bite. You ate a big slice!"

"I'm sorry I hid your new shoes."

"WHERE did you hide them?"

"I did jump on the bed."

"Beds are for sleeping—
not for jumping."

"And I accidentally broke
your favorite plate."

"This plate is in pieces.
Let's get the glue."

"I know I made some mistakes.
But please, Dad, don't be mad!"

"I'll even give you my special kite."

"You did not make me mad.
You don't need to give me your kite."

"It's no fun flying a kite alone. We can take your kite outside and fly it together!"

Word List (82 words)

(Words in **bold** have the silent *e* sound.)

a	did	I'm	more	slid
accidentally	don't	in	my	**slide**
alone	down	is	need	**some**
and	**even**	isn't	new	sorry
are	favorite	it	no	special
ate	fly	it's	not	**take**
be	flying	jump	of	than
bed	for	jumping	on	the
beds	fun	**kite**	**outside**	them
big	get	know	pieces	this
bit	give	let's	**plate**	to
bite	**glue**	mad	**please**	together
broke	guess	**made**	rail	we
but	hid	**make**	**shoes**	where
cake	**hide**	me	sleeping	you
can	I	**mistakes**	**slice**	your
Dad	I'll			

About the Author

A teacher for twenty years, Larry Dane Brimner is now a full-time writer who has penned more than 125 books for children, including several in the Rookie Reader series. Among his titles are *Nana's Hog*, *Nana's Fiddle*, and *Firehouse Sal*. He is also the author of the perennial favorites *Merry Christmas, Old Armadillo*, and *The Littlest Wolf*. He lives in Arizona's Old Pueblo.

About the Illustrator

Erin Eitter Kono has illustrated several picture books including *Nellie and the Bandit*, *Star Baby*, *Passover*, and *Hula Lullaby*, which she also wrote. She is the recipient of the Children's Literature Council's award for "Excellence in a Picture Book."